The Rewritten Word

How to Sculpt Literary Art,

No Matter the Genre

The Rewritten Word

How to Sculpt Literary Art,

No Matter the Genre

by

Aggie Villanueva

Cielos Rojos Publishing

ISBN 978-0-9825914-2-0

Printed in the United States of America.

What is written without effort is in general read without pleasure.

~ Samuel Johnson

Contents

Note to Readers

Before you begin reading, make sure to write an article or chapter or choose from something you've already written. You will apply the assignments at the end of each chapter to the same piece throughout.

This workbook is not how to produce en masse for submission to article directory engines, becoming an instant expert. That writing has its place, but I'm talking about how to rewrite until your work shines as literary art, fact or fiction, print or electronic.

Why is producing literary art so important? Because of The Reader. Everything is for The Reader. One sentence of verbose rambling can drive The Reader away. Readers are not only intelligent, but busy. Too busy to read 500 words when 200 would say it.

Some complain this busy lifestyle shackles the artistic bard. On the contrary, it demands writers take the time to polish work to precise perfection. This crafting of every word creates literary art. It demands less of the readers' time, much more of our own. Perhaps that's the root of our complaints.

Note about Examples Used Throughout

The art of the rewrite may be the most neglected aspect of writing, especially in this day of article submission directories. I use many examples throughout this book, all from talented and prolific published writers. I want to be clear that I'm not reproaching any writer's work. No prose is ever perfect, especially in the English language. There are always grammar, spelling, and style errors and every imaginable mistake. Believe me, you will find them in this book, too.

My purpose is to use hands-on examples from the best in the field and much from my own error-riddled writing to show that even professional writers need to practice the craft of the rewrite. We never get too good to improve our writing.

Each of my edits to their work demonstrates only one possible rewrite for example's sake. None imply I'm the better writer or that it should be done my way, but all illustrate the positive effects of rewriting. Each word eliminated or given wing (given active voice) is a step toward literary art. In the context of wading through hundreds of words per page, the elimination of but one unnecessary syllable is a boon that keeps our readers reading.

Introduction: Don't Taint My Talent

"But I don't want to sully my gift with rote education." Have you ever heard anyone say this? I have—even said similar things myself. And it's true to a point. You can't obtain talent through education. On the other hand, raw talent must learn everything about craft to know what to throw away and when. This is especially true with writing.

And rewriting is one of the most important aspects, contrary to some beliefs that rewriting means running a spelling and grammar checker. If you don't master the art of the rewrite, though you reek of raw talent, you'll never be paid for your prose.

The rewriting craft is like the familiar story where a city dweller admires the realistic horse carved by a man from the hills. The woodcarver waved away the compliments, explaining, "Shucks, I saw a horse in that piece of wood. All I did was cut away everything that ain't a horse."

The piece of wood was natural and pure, like raw talent, but it was just a piece of wood until the woodcarver took a knife to it. Only after he labored over it was it a piece of art. It's the same with writing.

Yes, we're given natural talent, that is, the ability to see a manuscript where none exists. But when we get this inspiration down on paper, it's only a piece of wood. We must labor over it, cutting away *what ain't a horse.*

Chop everything that prevents your readers' instantaneous comprehension and interest. Whittle away what buries the art of your words beneath pulp, no matter the topic, no matter the genre. We don't betray our gift when we put the knife to our writing. Rather, we sculpt our piece of wood.

When I first felt the call of writing, my response was to submit long, archaic poems and manuscripts in vast quantity. It never occurred to me to learn my craft first. I wrote articles explaining broad subjects, such as how to raise children. I never thought of sticking with a narrow topic until it was well covered. I had The Calling to write. I must be an expert on everything.

I resort to jest, but seriously, some shaking up had to happen before I took the responsibility for writing quality upon myself. Then I listened to writers and editors admonish: write, write, and rewrite. I heard and obeyed, but my final work was not much better than my rough draft. I soon discovered the reason. I didn't know what I was doing.

With my usual quick perception (and many rejected manuscripts, some of them nearly aflame from the speed with which they returned), I decided I needed some training. Reading books on the craft of writing, I was overwhelmed by what I didn't know. I signed up for courses, where I got my first real critical input. Community college classes provide a good form of objective criticism, as do online courses and forums. This type of critique is vital. Beginners simply don't have the knowledge to criticize their own work, and experienced writers always need fresh input.

Practice is critical, as is a grasp of grammar. But publication eludes without the constant use of learned skills. Even when we've fulfilled these career requirements, it is only the rewrite that polishes prose to perfection, if I may alliterate.

And if I may quote the Good Book, Ecclesiastes 5:7: "Much dreaming and many words are meaningless."

There is more to writing than putting many words to paper and more to rewriting than rearranging those words. Dreaming about writing won't get you anywhere, and writing a thousand words a day won't help unless you know what to do with those words.

THE REWRITTEN WORD

1

Lesson One: Organization—You Thought That Meant Outlining, Didn't You?

You've written a detailed outline and followed it with your first draft. You have your thoughts on paper—your piece of wood to carve into a work of literary art. You stand, knife at the ready, for the rewrite. But where to start?

Did I Include Everything?

There are many aspects to a well-organized piece. Usually around this point, I find I have left out some obvious element. For instance, after writing my draft for this chapter, I realized, with all my advice, I failed to give the hard-core how-tos of rewriting. A definite "Duh!" but more common than you think.

Go over your writing as if you don't know anything about the topic. What have you learned by reading it? Do you still have questions? Be sure your piece is complete.

Rambling

Do you say irrelevant things? Invariably I do. In the process of rewriting this chapter, I cut quite a bit about raising the quality of literature, a subject dear to my heart. That is a critical subject, but mine is rewriting.

This is the lead sentence from "The Importance of Writing High Quality Articles" (http://ezinearticles. com/?Article-Writing-Tips---The-Importance-of-Writing-High-Quality-Articles&id=1818736) by Fabian Tan, a prolific writer, but one who is as human as I am when it comes to the occasional oversight.

> One of the most brilliant things about the Internet is the ready availability of information on any chosen topic at nearly any time. I should have processed that statement by saying that this is a brilliant aspect of the Internet from the standpoint of the reader ...

Besides writers' common tendencies toward verbosity, this rambles. To first present the lead statement, and then say "I should have processed that statement" may confuse readers. Our statements should be processed before the reader sees them.

Try this as a possible way to a more organized thought.

> The ever-available information highway's reader benefits are brilliant.

Forty-six words cut to eight concise and clear words. And no information lost in the rewrite.

Clarity is Vital to Reader Comprehension

A big part of organizing your thoughts is clarity. Are there confusing sentence constructions like:

> Since there is no time like the present,
> he thought it was time to present the
> present.

I exaggerate, but sometimes we inadvertently make equally unclear or vague statements. Read through each sentence as if you didn't already know what you meant. You'll be amazed at what you find.

Clarity and conciseness go hand in hand, as illustrated by Philip Yaffe's article, "How Crafty Word Order Can Instantly Improve Your Writing" (http://www.articlesbase.com/non-fiction-articles/how-crafty-word-order-can-instantly-improve-your-writing-624229.html).

Philip Yaffe is a former reporter/feature writer with The Wall Street Journal and an international marketing communication consultant who now teaches courses in persuasive communication in Brussels, Belgium. Yaffe's newest book, *In the "I" of the Storm: the Simple Secrets of Writing & Speaking (Almost) like a Professional*, was released a few years ago.

EXCERPT: HOW CRAFTY WORD ORDER CAN INSTANTLY IMPROVE YOUR WRITING
(http://www.articlesbase.com/non-fiction-articles/how-crafty-word-order-can-instantly-improve-your-writing-624229.html)

Clarity. For your text to be truly clear, you must:

1. Emphasize what is of primary importance.
2. De-emphasize what is of secondary importance.
3. Eliminate what is of no importance.

Conciseness. For your text to be truly concise, you must ensure that it is:

1. As long as necessary.
2. As short as possible.

Organization also means to arrange the words in each sentence to create the most logical flow that also packs the most punch. Organize your sentences to captivate. Again, I will excerpt from Philip Yaffe's article. He has summarized how to do this better than anyone I've read.

Fully benefit from the two hotspots in each and every sentence you write.

Hotspots? Yes. You may never have noticed it, but words at the beginning and at the end of a sentence have stronger emphasis than those in the middle. Therefore, by putting important information in these key locations, you aid reader comprehension.

Here's an example to demonstrate how hotspots work. While considering the following three sentences, bear in mind that hotspots don't have equal value. In general, the one at the end of a sentence is somewhat more forceful than the one at the beginning.

A. Astronomers hunting for evidence of life outside of our solar system announced discovery of a new class of planets yesterday.

B. Yesterday astronomers hunting for evidence of life outside of our solar system announced discovery of a new class of planets.

C. Astronomers hunting for evidence of life outside of our solar system yesterday announced discovery of a new class of planets.

I hope you will agree that sentence A says what it has to say. But sentence B is rather better. And sentence C is best of all. Why?

In A, we see that "yesterday", the time of the announcement, is in the hotspot at the end of the sentence. However, knowing when the announcement was made is hardly as important as the announcement itself. Moving "yesterday" to the hotspot at the beginning in sentence B somewhat helps, but the time of the announcement is still very much a detail.

Sentence C puts "yesterday" in the middle, where such a minor detail belongs. This leaves the hotspots at the beginning and end free to convey truly key information.

Let's look at another example.

A. The national leaders met to discuss new trade relations between their two countries in the Royal Palace.

B. In the Royal Palace the national leaders met to discuss new trade relations between their two countries.

C. The national leaders met in the Royal Palace to discuss new trade relations between their two countries.

Here, the disturbing minor element is the phrase "in the Royal Palace". Once again we see that moving it from the end of A to the beginning of B is an improvement. However, putting it in the middle of C is best of all.

Always think of your reader. How does it sound to him? How does it flow for her? Can they understand it in one quick reading? Does one concise thought compel them quickly and smoothly to the next? If reader comprehension is sluggish in one sentence, they usually won't bother to read the next.

Thank you, Mr. Yaffe, for this excellent lesson.

Organization: Too Much of A Good Thing?

Just because you followed an outline doesn't mean you achieved organization—not yet. There is more to organization than logical sequence. Read through your piece again as if you've never seen it before. If you're like me, you may find it choppy, jerky, and, excuse the four-letter word, but it's a B-O-R-E. Poor organization always makes for boring reading.

One of the best organizational tips I've found is that you can usually start your piece about one-third of the way into it. Many editors tell me they routinely cut the first one to three paragraphs of an article without even reading them, and it nearly always improves the work.

That may seem unwarranted, especially staring into your inspired words, each more beautiful than the last. I didn't believe it either until it happened to me.

For a year, I'd researched and outlined my second novel, Rightfully Mine (http://www.amazon.com/Rightfully-Mine-Equal-Rights-Amendment/dp/055708654X/ref=sr_1_2?ie=UTF8&s=books&qid=1285941188&sr=1-2), published by Thomas Nelson (http://www.thomasnelson.com/consumer/), 1986. All my groundwork laid, all the prep work finished, I finally wrote my proposal, the first three chapters and an outline of the rest. Teaching at a conference in Minnesota, I was excited to meet with one of my mentors, who was also teaching there.

Tom Noton, then editor of *The Christian Writer*, had accepted several of my articles and even featured my co-author and me on the cover. We met for lunch the first day, and I gave him my proposal to critique.

The following day we met again for lunch and made small talk. Then he tossed my manuscript in front of me saying, "Rewrite it." My heart sank, but I wanted honesty.

What I also got was one of the greatest compliments an editor can give. He had enough faith in my writing ability, but most importantly my perseverance, to not tell me how to rewrite it. He fully expected me to figure it out.

After my last class of the day, I bee-lined for my room and read my proposal through as if I'd never seen it before. Mr. Noton was right. It was sluggish, verbose, meandering, and not the least bit riveting. Through the night I cut away until I realized that chapter three was actually chapter one.

Perusing chapter three as if it were the beginning, I discovered it indeed stood on its own, with the exception of needing a handful of sentences to explain something from the first two chapters. I cut two-thirds of my manuscript and couldn't even tell — except now it read powerfully and smoothly and grabbed interest from the first sentence. I showed it to Tom the next day and he laughed and said, "Now you got it! I knew you would." With those rewrites, the first publisher I sent it to accepted it.

First Two Paragraphs of Rightfully Mine

It was inconceivable that after forty years of chastisement in the Zin desert and the recent military successes in the Transjordan hills, the wandering nation of Israel could succumb to the temptations offered by the Moabite and Midianite women, but the tomb-like encampment attested to the sin. As a result, hundreds and thousands of sprawling black tents suffocated their inhabitants with the lingering, putrid taste of the death within them.

The vast camp of Israel lay crippled by plague. They huddled piteously beneath arcing acacia branches along the oasis-like steam of Abel Shittim, the only shelter available in the scorching summer sands of the Moab plains. Israel was halted only a few miles east of the Jordan they yearned to cross.

Assignment: Organization

1. Concentrating on nothing but inclusion, go through your article applying this lesson's rewriting principle of inclusion. Get in a quiet place where you can ask yourself the inclusion questions without interruption and add to your article accordingly. If you've left nothing out, good for you. If all you need to add is one explanatory sentence, wonderful. Don't feel you must add if it's not needed.

2. For the inclusion rewrite, go over your piece as if you don't know anything about the topic. What have you learned by reading it? Do you still have questions? Be sure your piece is complete.

3. Check for rambling. Read through your article again. Delete anything that doesn't pertain to the topic at hand.

4. Clarity. Read through your article again. Tag any sentences/paragraphs not crystal clear upon the first reading. Pretend you don't know what you meant and that you can only understand from what you say.

5. Make sure you don't have too much of a good thing. Can you scratch one to three of your first paragraphs (or middle) without losing anything? Does the fourth or more paragraph/sentence have the opening zing you want? Then start there, rearranging/inserting information to conform to this.

Lesson Two: Verboten Verbosity

Though you have a great article idea and/or are an experienced writer, I hope you're seeing your words still need to be polished. This reality usually comes after the glow of inspiration: the piece is verbose, a cardinal writing sin. That's okay. At least you have your *piece of wood* in hand.

When a friend asked me to help decipher important prescriptions warnings, this is what we faced.

Excerpted from *Indications and Usage*, included with the prescription.

> There have been reports of hepatic failure, sometimes fatal ...increased the risk of elevation of serum transaminases levels in development program clinical trials. Liver transaminase elevations resulted in the discontinuation of 0.3% (82/27, 229) of treated patients. In these patients, the median time to detection of the transaminase elevation was about two months.

Admittedly this is an extreme example, but this is how vital information about our prescriptions is written. What if you were one of the 0.3% that are "sometimes fatal" and your warnings were lost in meaningless jabber?

Checking my own first drafts for wordiness, I cut probably half my words. Does that mean I'm a poor writer? Could be, but perhaps, instead, it shows I care about what lands on an editor's desk with my name attached. I care even more about my readers.

Every unnecessary word cut gives the reader better understanding. If they have to re-read even one sentence to understand it, you've lost them. Your ideas can't flow unimpeded if your words don't. Unblock the flow of words by shortening them.

Here is a sentence as it was originally written for this article:

> That is a vital subject to writers, but I am writing a book about rewriting, and though I did tie in the need for excellent quality writing, my main recourse must be the specific area of perfecting our work: rewriting.

The same sentence after the knife:

> That is a critical subject, but mine is rewriting.

I cut the sentence from 40 words to nine without losing any meaning. Most of the words were repeats. If you lean towards verbosity, as I do, this phase of the rewriting craft is imperative.

Another of my sentences (19 words) before rewriting:

> Use a thesaurus to make your meaning clearer, not to amaze readers with your knowledge of big words.

Substitute four words (knowledge of big words) for one: intelligence. Then cut a few unneeded words and now its 14 words smoothly read:

> Use a thesaurus to make your meaning clear, not to amaze with your intelligence.

The following paragraph (73 words) is from "Government Business Grants for Small Business Start-Ups" (http://www.articlesbase.com/fundraising-articles/government-business-grants-for-small-business-start-ups-658458.html), by Andrew Bicknell, a prolific writer at www.ArticleBase.com:

> It is important that you use any grant money you receive for the purpose for which you originally stated in your application and business plan. Those agencies that granted the money for your business purposes want to see you succeed. They believe you have a sound plan but if you are found not to be using the money to further your success you stand a good chance of being strongly sanctioned or penalized.

Are these 35 words easier to grasp?

> Your granting agencies want to see you succeed, so be sure to use their money as stated in your application and business plan. Honor their belief in you.

> Dishonesty risks strong sanctions or penalties.

Lead paragraph to "3 Simple Methods to Improve Your Writing" (http://ezinearticles.com/?Article-Writing---3-Simple-Methods-to-Improve-Your-Writing&id=1813399), by Sharon and Larry Zolna, expert writers who, like all of us, can sometimes use too many words—73 words.

> Advertising costs for your website can be very expensive. However, Article Writing not only is a great way to get traffic but it is also free! By writing quality articles that are filled with good, informative content you will advance as an expert in your field. Article Writing will therefore increase your traffic to your Squeeze Page or Website with readers who are interested in your topic and are not just tire kickers.

Let's try it like this:

> Advertising costs continue to skyrocket. Speed free traffic to your website with Article Writing. Quality, content-matched articles both increase interested traffic and establish your expertise.

No detail omitted, but at 26 words, down from 73, reader comprehension and interest increased.

Also note an error in style made in the title. According to my old Strunk Elements of Style, numbers one through nine should be spelled out; from 10 up you may use numerals. I assume this style rule is ignored for directory listings because alphabetically numbers are listed before the letter a.

Opening to "Tips to Get Your Ex-Girlfriend Back for Good" (http://www.amazines.com/Relationships/article_detail. cfm?articleid=721091) by relationship expert Gerry Restrivera.

> You probably feel down that she is gone and still figuring out how to get your ex girlfriend back for good. You've been trying to reach her but the more you try the more she avoids you. This is really a nerve-racking situation and of course you want to find out the best way to get her back.
>
> Everybody deserves a second chance to enjoy a beautiful relationship with someone they love. Once you realized that you are miserable without her, it is also a realization that you need to get your ex girlfriend back for good. Here are some tips to win her back:

A possible rewrite, reducing the number of words from 105 to 38, with simplified sentences:

> You're miserable without her. She's avoiding you since the breakup. Your nerves frazzled, you rack your brain for the best way to win her back, because everyone deserves a second chance. Try these tips to re-win her heart.

Again, nothing lost that was said in the original, but a great gain in flow and reader comprehension.

Assignment: Verboten Verbosity

1. Go through each paragraph of your piece as if you are distracted. Remember, most readers are. They only pay close attention if your grab it and refuse to let it go.

2. Does a sentence or paragraph seem to run on?

3. Is the thought of each one crystal clear using as few words as possible?

4. Are most of your sentences short?

5. As you go, correct each sentence that doesn't conform.

Lesson Three: Actively Rewrite—Active Voice vs. Passive/Past Tense vs. Present

There are tomes written about the weakness of passive voice. This principle underscores every written word, particularly every rewritten word. Though passive voice is unavoidable, using active whenever possible improves your writing.

Run your grammar checker to see how many passive phrases it flags. Not a foolproof method by any means, and not one to rely on. Only you can find them all and make the judgment, but this will flag some examples to watch for and alert you to how often you write in passive voice. The present tense, rather than past, also dulls your writing

Excerpted from an article I recently edited, written by an extremely talented writer of technical manuscripts, one of the most difficult genres to make active.

> **ME:**
> In your first paragraph I've highlighted in red the weak, or passive, words to avoid. When you use these words they force you

to construct a weak, inactive sentence. (Like the passive sentence I just wrote using the words *when, you, they.*)

The first words of a sentence can make or break it. Change my passive sentence above to begin with the word *use,* which is active (rather than *When you use*), and you force a construction something like this: "Use these words to construct a weak, inactive sentence." That's the active voice. Of course, passive words must be used occasionally, but unless absolutely necessary eliminate them.

THE WRITER'S PARAGRAPH:
White balance is a system by which your camera measures the 'temperature' of the available light in your scene, and it will have either a warm or cool effect on the outcome of your photos. Ideally, the correct setting should match the color temperature of your light source so that your photos have the right colors to your eye.

ME:
Compare your paragraph with this possible rewrite:

Want to give photos a hot snap, or ice them down? White balance measures your camera's light "temperature." Want to record colors the same way your eye sees them? Set your white balance to match the color temperature of its light source. It's easy, if you understand a few white balance basics.

At times I used modifiers like *the*, but see how much faster it now reads and how much quicker the reader understands, which translates to "Hmm, I think I'll read more." The active voice hooks 'em and lands 'em.

One word is always better than two. Compare: *I slowly moved* to *I inched*. Instead of using two words (slowly, moved), one a passive adverb, use one active descriptive verb, such as inched.

Beware the First Person

Unless the writer is another Truman Capote, first person narratives are usually verbose, choppy, and unnatural-sounding to the reading ear.

There are many drawbacks, and a major one is the number of times present tense/first person uses the word *I*. The word *I* reminds the reader they are not really there; you are. Eliminate as many *I*'s as possible.

This paragraph used 73 words, the word *I* seven times. Present tense makes it mostly passive voice. The writer attempted first person present tense narrative, but unintentionally switched back and forth, using past tense more often than present:

> Never fearing I might get lost, I just continued *(past tense)* to move in a direction that took me *(past tense)* around the west and north side of the peak. I stumbled *(past tense)* across a set of white washed and pitted elk bones. Mostly undisturbed, I studied (past tense) them – they had been there

a long time and I left them **(past tense: present would read: leave them)** as I found them. Animals will chew **(future tense)** on them for food and calcium. I shoot **(present tense) a picture to remember.**

An example of how quickly and easily we can switch from verbosity and passive voice, here is how it could be rewritten to flow actively in past tense/third person.

Resolutely, I continued west and north of the peak until stumbling across a pitted, whitewashed elk skeleton, mostly undisturbed. I studied the bones. Leaving them as found, so animals could chew on them for food and calcium, I shot a picture to remember.

The word *I* used three times, as opposed to seven, with fewer passive words and phrases, and only 43 words, compared to 73.

First person also forces an even more passive voice than usual. It's hard to find a manuscript where first person narrative/present tense is done smoothly, actively, and unobtrusively.

Spend a few hours reading writer's guidelines for publications. I came across several online that instructed "no first person narratives. Always submit articles written in third person." This made me realize publishing hasn't changed much in the last 25 years. Rules of good writing seldom change.

-Ly & -Ing Words

Cut words ending with *ly* as much as possible, so your adverbs will add punch when you do use them. They are a great tool, but when overused promote a jerky flow, as in this published sentence from my novel *Chase the Wind* (http://www.alibris.co.uk/search/books/author/Villanueva,%20Aggie), coauthored with Deborah Lawrence, Thomas Nelson, 1983.

> He patted her hand and smiled sympa-
> thetically, but to Gomer his lips curved
> grotesquely and his lowered voice
> sounded more like a hiss than a whisper.

The adverb *sympathetically* is, in this case, unnecessary since patting a hand is a universal sympathetic gesture. The adverb *grotesquely* is also unnecessary since a lowered voice sounding more like a hiss than a whisper is grotesque. Besides being unnecessary, notice how the adverbs chop the flow compared to this:

> He patted her hand and smiled, but to
> Gomer his lowered voice sounded more
> like a hiss than a whisper.

Nothing lost in the rewrite, but great punch gained. Never underestimate the intellect of the reader. No need to overstate or overwrite to get the point across.

Words ending with *ing* also stir choppy literary waters when overused, as in this sentence.

> For a year, I'd been researching and
> outlining my second novel.

The following seems a small, but evident improvement in the active voice. But not so small when multiplied hundreds of times throughout an article, eliminating hundreds of unnecessary words.

> For a year, I'd researched and outlined
> my second novel.

The passive researching and outlining reads much smoother in a more active form. Don't leave readers adrift. Don't make them work for comprehension. Writing in the active voice naturally propels sentences and thoughts forward. Launch readers into your word flow, and guide them with a concise rudder.

Assignment: Actively Rewrite

1. Go over your piece yet again, this time looking only for cases where you use passive voice. It's not always possible, but where it is, switch to active.

2. Edit your weak sentences to begin with an active word.

3. Can you turn three or four word phrases into one or two word phrases?

4. Eliminate the word *I* as much as possible.

5. Do you use too many words ending in *ing*?

6. Eliminate unneeded words ending in *ly*.

7. Go over your piece yet again, this time focusing on finding and correcting cases where you've switched tenses from past to present or vice-versa. Be consistent.

4

Lesson Four: Lightning and the Lightning Bug—Write the Right Words

Circle all words that aren't to the point. The thesaurus is invaluable here. I use it to find words saying precisely what I mean, and in some cases I can substitute one perfect word for five weak ones. Mark Twain said that "the difference between the almost right word & the right word is the difference between the lightning bug and the lightning." As helpful as the thesaurus is, it is abused by those who try to emulate archaic writers who use exotic words.

Have you ever read a sentence like this?

> Humanity is conceived here exclusively in terms of ritual function—man is made in order to offer sacrifices to the gods— and so the highly differentiated realms of history and moral action are not intimated in the account of man's creation.

Wouldn't it make more sense like this?

According to this account of man's creation, our only function is to sacrifice to the gods. The many facets of our purpose, such as our varied history and morality, are not even hinted at.

My edit may not impress the intelligentsia, but I understood it. Use a thesaurus to make your meaning clear, not to amaze with your intelligence.

In my second novel, *Rightfully Mine,* published by Thomas Nelson 1986, I had one sentence to set a foreboding, isolated mood and transmit mundane information. Many months had passed since the previous chapter, so I had to establish the setting without losing the urgency of the action.

Using my thesaurus through I don't know how many verbose rewrites, it took three days to achieve success. I didn't save those drafts, but this rewrite ended up in the book:

> The partial moon's spectral lucency
> darted over tiny crevices that were
> already stretching the thirsty plain
> asunder with the late spring drought.

Were I editing that sentence today, it would read:

> The partial moon's spectral lucency
> darted over tiny crevices that already
> stretched the thirsty plain asunder with
> the late spring drought.

Seemingly minor differences, but multiplied by tens of thousands of words these rewrites make vast reading enhancements. The difference between the right word and the almost right word is the difference between lightning and the lightning bug.

Using my first draft of this book to illustrate once again, here's another paragraph before my rewrite.

> I can't remember how many times I rewrote it using my thesaurus, but I know after many drafts that each dragged on for several sentences, I had to come back to it three days straight before I succeeded. I don't have those drafts, but this is the rewrite that ended up in the book:

The rewrite:

> Using my thesaurus through I don't know how many verbose rewrites, it took three days to achieve success. I didn't save those drafts, but this rewrite ended up in the book:

The original: 54 words, the word *I* used six times. The rewrite: 31 words, *I* used twice. Among the many other cuts, I substituted *many verbose rewrites* for *many drafts that each dragged on for several sentences.* Less is always more for your readers.

Titles are a great exercise in finding the perfect word. You can't waste a syllable. I put much thought into titling my photographic art. Here's an example from my own workflow, conception to creation, using my thesaurus throughout.

I want the title to convey some kind of benevolent guardian from ancient times through to a future we can't foresee or even imagine.

Beyond the Horizon
Beyond Tomorrow
Beyond Benevolence
Encounter the Beyond
Echo Range
Echo Encounter
Shadow Echo (Shadows)
Esprit Echoes
Echo Outpost
Rim
Beyond, span, yonder, yon, hereafter, remote, distant, outpost
Icy
Outpost, station, post, paradisal, frontier, tower, defense, scout, guard, watch
comfort, cozy
abandoned, depleted, ghostly, spectral, wraith, shrouded, macabre
Phantom Outpost
Phantom Dispatch
Phantom Point
Phantom Repose
Outpost Shroud
Paradise's Outpost
Eden's Outpost
Vigilante Paradise
Millennial Outpost

Millennial Outpost it is. Remember my first summary sentence stating what I wanted to convey with my title? The word *millennial* infers godliness and benevolence at the same time it projects from an ancient past to a distant future.

Outpost conveys guardianship and hints at this benevolence standing guard for us from times before and in
dangerous frontiers. It took me hours to get two perfect words to convey all that, but it was worth it.

The importance of perfectly worded titles can get lost in
our keyword-conscious virtual world. My fine art title
above would never serve this purpose. Literary art has
given way to search engine optimization. This is actually the title of an article that was at one time on www.
ArticlesBase.com (no byline available): "Desktop Pen
Stand, Pen Holder, Folding Pen Stand, Card Holder,
Office Desk Set, Ball Pen Stands, Wooden Pen Stand."

'Nuff said.

Assignment: Lightning and the Lightning Bug

1. Circle all words in your piece that aren't to the point.

2. Use a thesaurus to simplify your words, not to sound more intelligent.

3. Having a hard time finding the right word? Think about exactly what you want to convey in the word. What kind of emotion? The *exact* meaning(s).

Lesson Five: A Few Facts on Fiction— Everything We've Just Covered, but Related to Fiction Only

Dialogue, Plotting, and Characterization Rewrites

We've covered many things to consider when rewriting, but fiction has some unique aspects. Mostly you want to use simple, short, flowing words to pull the reader along. But at times, like when you set a mood, each word must propel them; waste one and break the spell.

These rewriting excerpts from my first historical novel, *Chase the Wind*, coauthored with Deborah Lawrence, published by Thomas Nelson 1983, exemplify that everything we've covered applies to fiction — and then some.

FIRST DRAFT:

There is nothing you can do to me now, lord of Israel. If you slay me on this spot you would not have the satisfaction of seeing my obedience. No torture would induce the desired action in me. I will perform for you no longer.

Though my characters are circa 900 B.C., this was still way too wordy and meandering. Not sure what the problem was, I tried again.

FIRST REWRITE:

Do you think this is the way to fight for a woman? You took my husband. Your threats are useless now. There is nothing more you can do to me, lord of Israel. By your own tactics you have lost this war.

SECOND REWRITE: Notice I kept adding information:

Do you think this is the way to fight for a woman, you silly suckling? Your threats are useless now, for you have taken my husband. There is nothing more you can do to me, lord of Israel. All your power over me is drained, for you have uncorked my reserve of wine; my husband. Though I leave him, I love him. But now I will perform for you no longer. By your own tactics you have lost this war.

THIRD REWRITE:

Do you think this is the way to fight for a woman, by taking away her husband?

Though I left him, I loved him. You
have lost all power over me, for there is
nothing more you can do to me. Your
threats are useless now. By your own
tactics you have lost this war.

FINAL REWRITE:

There is nothing more you can do to hurt
me. Your threats are useless now, lord of
Israel. By your own tactics you lost this
war.

Why was the last rewrite so short? Struggling over this
paragraph, I realized people don't give soliloquies in
the midst of angry outbursts.

Continuing to hack away, I sensed half the things this
character said were unnecessary. I had only included
them so the reader would know what was going on. I
needed to clarify my plot, not lengthen my dialogue.

Still, I could not figure out how to make her inferences
about the war between them clear without her explaining it. I went back through my manuscript. It turned
out I had to strengthen my characterizations in preced-
ing chapters. Then the reader would be aware of the
rivalry between these two without a stream of unreal-
istic dialogue.

Without continual scrutiny of my own words, I would
not have known what was wrong, much less how to
correct it. If you haven't gone over each of your words
until you are utterly sick of them, you haven't suffi-
ciently scrutinized your work. It's much less painful

to complete the rewriting process now than to suffer continual editorial rejection, or worse, make reading your work a chore when it should be a pleasure.

One last note. Even after your careful and extensive rewriting, don't resist an editor's every edit. They drop writers who challenge them, unless it's a factual mistake. Editors have numerous reasons behind each edit, but not the time or the inclination to defend them. They are certainly not gods, but we can't fathom all their reasons, some as simple as house preference.

If I don't understand editors' edits (which was often as a beginner), I ask them why they made the change in the way they made it. I don't challenge the changes, just ask to understand them.

Editors appreciate when you want to learn, not protect your writing from them. This is possible only if the editor is open to dialogue. Many are not. With the exception of an actual incorrect fact, editors are always right, as is the proverbial customer.

When an editor takes the time to write out the reasons for an edit, there is no higher praise, even if it's only a few words. One of the reasons I sell is that I understand my pages are not etched in stone.

By the time I'm done with this book, I will have rewritten extensively at least ten times. This may sound like a lot of work, and it may be extreme compared to other writers, but for me it's necessary to produce a worthy manuscript.

Maybe someday, when I have enough study and practice behind me, I will be able to cut that down to three or four. For now, I'll continue to work hard at writing and be thankful that, after the rewrites, I have a manuscript an editor is willing to pay for. And, when you vitalize your words with artful rewrites, you will too. I look forward to seeing your literary art on the market soon, no matter the topic, no matter the genre.

Additional Resources

You may want to contact the authors before downloading from unfamiliar sites. Please use your best judgment on the offers below. Listing here is not necessarily a recommendation.

The Impotence of Proofreading Video.

http://www.youtube.com/
watch?v=OonDPGwAyfQ

The Frugal Editor by Carolyn Howard-Johnson.

http://www.amazon.com/gp/product/0978515870

Editing Primer by Lillie Ammann.

http://lillieammann.com/books/editing-primer

"Rewriting Made Easy" by K.M. Weiland.

http://wordplay-kmweiland.blogspot.com/2010/02/rewriting-made-easy.html

"How to Brutalize Your Work" by Roscoe Barnes III.

http://www.absolutewrite.com/novels/brutalize_work.htm

Promotion á la Carte, an innovative, budget minded menu of author promotional services.

http://www.promotionalacarte.com

Visual Arts Junction, where you can learn all about how to promote your own writing.

http://www.visualartsjunction.com

Author Biography

Aggie Villanueva

Writing since the late 70's, bestselling author Aggie Villanueva's first novel, *Chase the Wind*, was published by Thomas Nelson in 1983, and *Rightfully Mine* was published, also by Thomas Nelson, in 1986.

Villanueva is also a critically acclaimed photographic artist (http://www.aggiev.org) represented by galleries nationwide, including Xanadu Gallery in Scottsdale, AZ (http://www.xanadugallery.com/Art/ArtistGallery.asp?ArtistID=429). Villanueva freelanced throughout the 80s and 90s, also writing three craft columns and three software review columns for national magazines. She was featured on the cover of *The Christian Writer Magazine* in October 1983.

For decades peers have described Aggie as a whirlwind that draws others into her vortex. And no wonder. She was a published author at Thomas Nelson before she was 30 and commenced to found local writers' groups including the Mid-America Fellowship of Christian Writers three–day conference, taught at nationwide writing conferences, and published numerous writing newsletters for various organizations. Over the years she has worked on professional product launches with the likes of Denise Cassino (http://www.wizardlywebdesigns.com), a foremost Joint Venture Specialist in the area of book launches.

Aggie founded Visual Arts Junction blog (http://www.visualartsjunction.com) in February 2009 and by the end of the same year, it was voted #5 at Preditors & Editors in the category "Writers' Resource, Information & News Source" for 2009 (http://www.critters.org/predpoll/final_tally_writerinfo.ht).

Now, under the Visual Arts Junction umbrella, Aggie has launched Promotion á la Carte (http://www.promotionalacarte.com), author promotional services where, guided by her experience and organizational/marketing savvy, authors gain the most promotional bang for their buck.

For more information you can contact Villanueva at aggie@promotionalacarte.com or go directly to Promotion á la Carte (http://www.promotionalacarte.com).

Learn More at the Author's Websites:

Aggie Villanueva, Grandma Moses of
the Southwest

http://www.aggiev.org

Promotion á la Carte

http://www.promotionalacarte.com

Visual Arts Junction

http://www.visualartsjunction.com